Mason J

Amazingly Healthy And Delicious Recipes For Salads On The Go

Sara Banks

Symbol LLC

Table Of Contents

⍰

Introduction

I want to thank you and congratulate you for purchasing the book "Mason Jar Salads- Amazingly Healthy And Delicious Recipes For Salads On The Go"

Like Most people you probably live a pretty busy life and often resort to fast food or the vending machine for your snacks and meals throughout the day. While this may be convenient for you it is no doubt very unhealthy. I want to show you how you can eat healthier while on the go by using simple mason jars. People all over are eating healthy while on the go and you can to. I have some fantastic salad recipes that I know you will just love.

Inside this recipe book you will get my best salad recipes that are not only delicious but also much healthier for you than the vending machine. I am really excited to share these with you!

Thanks again!

Sara Banks

Having some nice fresh salad over lunch at work with your vegetables still nice and crunchy is simply amazing. Most people don't usually carry salads to work due to improper packing that leads to the vegetables being soaked with the dressing. One of the reasons that I somehow stopped carrying salads for lunch was the mess the salad dressing would make once I packed my lunch box and put it in my bag. However, once I learnt about packing salads in a mason jar, I am no longer afraid of making a mess.

You may probably be wondering of what use a mason jar can be. The amazing thing about a mason jar is that you can layer the vegetables adequately and once you cover the jar with your lid, you don't have to worry about spillage. Furthermore, if you pack the jar adequately, you don't need to worry about your vegetables being soggy. In addition, since mason jars are usually made of glass, you don't have to worry about the food reacting with the glass and releasing some toxic materials as in the case of plastics. The amazing thing about mason jar salads is that once you seal the jar properly, you can store the salad up to seven days when chilled. How amazing is that. Thus, you can make several salads and have something different to carry to work daily for lunch.

When choosing a jar, ensure that you choose one that has a wide mouth as this one is easier to fill with whatever ingredients. You can also eat your salad from a wide-mouthed jar so no need to put the salad on a plate or bowl. We will have a look at some of the amazing and mason jar salads so that you can get started on preparing your mason jar salads.

Salads Group #1

Chicken Taco Salad

Servings: 4

What you need

1 cup of chopped romaine lettuce

1 cup of diced tomatoes

1 cup of canned corn

1 cup of canned black beans

2 whole grilled chicken breasts

4 (12-ounce) mason jars

Creamy avocado dressing

1 whole avocado

¼ cup of water

¼ teaspoon salt

¼ teaspoon of cumin

Juice of one lime

¼ cup of fresh cilantro

2 ounces of crumbled goat cheese

¼ cup of Greek yoghurt

Directions

Dressing directions

Mix the Greek yoghurt, cilantro, goat cheese, lime juice, salt, cumin, avocado and water in a food processor. Puree in a food processor until the mixture is smooth and preserve it. Cut the grilled chicken into small pieces using a fork.

Arrange each Mason jar in the order given below:

Bottom layer: ¼ cup of the avocado dressing

Second bottom layer: ¼ cup of corn

Third: ¼ cup of the black beans

Fourth: ¼ cup of the diced tomatoes

Fifth layer: ½ cup of chicken

Sixth layer: ¼ cup of the romaine lettuce

Put in the refrigerator until when ready to eat.

Fresh Mozzarella, Spinach, and Tomato Salad

Servings: 5

What you need

10 cups of baby spinach

2 cups of dry whole grain cooked pasta

10 ounces of fresh Mozzarella

1 quart grape tomatoes

10 tablespoons of balsamic vinegar dressing

5 quart size mason salad jars

Directions

Split the ingredients uniformly in mason jars. Start with your dressing followed by tomatoes, Mozzarella, pasta, and finish off with the spinach. Close tightly with the lid. Shake the jar to coat the dressing and put in the refrigerator until when you want to eat but ensure that it does not exceed 5 days.

Mediterranean Bean Salad In A Jar

Servings: 4

What you need

1 cup of diced tomato

1 cup of diced cucumber

1 cup of canned black beans (drained and rinsed)

1 cup of canned cannellini beans (drained and rinsed)

2 cups of canned garbanzo beans (drained and rinsed)

1 cup of cooked Israeli couscous

4 (12-ounce) mason jars

1 cup feta cheese, crumbed

Garlic and lemon dressing

Salt and pepper to taste

2 tablespoons of olive oil

1 whole minced garlic clove

2 tablespoons of finely chopped shallots

Juice and zest of two lemons

Directions

Dressing preparation

Combine the salt, pepper, olive oil, garlic, shallots, zest and lemon juice in a small bowl.

Whisk the contents until they are thoroughly combined. Set them aside.

Arrange each of the mason jars in the order below:

1st layer (bottom): put 3 tablespoons of lemon garlic dressing

2nd layer: add ¼ cup of cucumber

3rd layer: ½ cup of garbanzo

4th layer: ¼ cup of tomatoes, diced

5th layer: ¼ cup of cannelli beans

6th layer: ¼ cup of black beans

7th layer: ¼ cup of couscous

8th layer: ¼ cup of feta cheese

When you are done refrigerate the salads until when you ready to eat.

Veggie, Goat Cheese and Chicken Mason Jar Salad

Servings: 5

What you need

10 ounce of arugula package

1 ¼ cup of shredded rotisserie chicken

5 ounces of crumbled goat cheese

1 ¼ cup of cooked whole grain spiral pasta

1 chopped red onion

5 bell peppers (chopped and seeded)

1 quart of cherry tomatoes (halved)

10 tablespoons of olive oil and vinegar dressing

5 wide mouth quart sized mason salad jars

Directions

Assemble the Mason jars and split the ingredients between the jars. Begin from the bottom with dressing then followed by the tomatoes, the peppers, the onions, pasta, the goat cheese, the chicken and finally end with the arugula at the top. Refrigerate the salad then shake the jar and pour into a bowl when ready to eat.

Creamy Citrus Chicken and Orzo Salad in A Jar

Servings: 4

What you need

2 cups of fresh spinach

1 cup of chopped red onion

2 whole diced roasted red peppers

1 whole grilled chicken breast

2 cups of cooked orzo

4 (12 ounce) mason jars

Creamy citrus dressing

2 tablespoons of olive oil

1 teaspoon of balsamic vinegar

1 ½ teaspoons of orange zest

¼ cup of orange juice

2 tablespoons of Greek yoghurt

Salt and pepper to taste

Directions

Dressing

Mix the orange zest, Greek yoghurt, orange juice, balsamic vinegar, salt, olive oil and pepper in a small bowl. Whisk them well until combined evenly. Shred the grilled chicken into small pieces.

Arrange the mason jars in the order below:

1st layer (bottom): 3 tablespoons of creamy citrus dressing

2nd layer: ½ cup of roasted red peppers

3rd layer: ¼ cup of red onions

4th layer: ½ cup of orzo

5th layer: ¼ cup of shredded chicken

Sixth layer: ¼ cup of spinach

Store in the refrigerator until when you are ready to eat.

Deconstructed California Roll

Servings: 4

What you need

1 cup of lump crab meat (picked)

4 whole nori sheets (cut into small pieces)

2 whole cucumbers (peeled, seeded and diced)

2 tablespoons lemon juice

2 whole avocados

1 tablespoon soy sauce

1 teaspoon of sugar

1 tablespoon of rice vinegar

2 cups white or brown rice (cooked)

4 (12-ounce) mason jars

Directions

In a small saucepan, heat the vinegar and sugar until the sugar has dissolved. Pour the vinegar and soy sauce over the rice while the rice is still warm. Toss it to combine and let it cool down.

Brush avocado with lemon juice as the rice cools down. Layer the salad as shown below:

First layer (bottom): ½ cup of rice

Second layer: ½ cup of cucumber

Third layer: 1 nori sheet (cut into small pieces)

Fourth layer: ¼ cup of crab

Fifth layer (top): ½ avocado

Close the jar tightly and store in the refrigerator until you are ready to eat.

Salads Group #2

Mediterranean Chickpea Salad

Servings: 3

Ingredients

A handful of raisins

½ cup of black olives

1 cup of cucumber, chopped

1 cup of red pepper, chopped

1 large lemon

½ can of chickpeas

¼ cup of chopped red onions

1 garlic clove chopped finely

Spinach

Directions

Chickpea marinade

Dice the lemon into two haves and juice one-half only.

Combine chickpeas, garlic, lemon juice and red onion in a medium sized bowl.

Put the combination in a jar in the order below:

Layer 1: marinated chickpeas

Layer 2: red pepper and cucumber

Layer 3: olives

Layer 4: raisins

Layer 5: spinach

While serving, squeeze the remaining half of the lemon to extract the juice into the salad.

Quinoa Salad in Jar

Servings: 4

What you need

1 cup of grapes or any other fruits

1 cup of packed spinach leaves

1 cup of chopped tomatoes

1 cup of broccoli (chopped)

1 can of kidney beans (rinsed and drained)

½ cup of red onions (chopped)

½ cup of chopped olives

1 cup of quinoa (cooked)

4 mason jars

Directions

Put together the quinoa with olives and onions and split among the jars, with the quinoa at the bottom. Divide the kidney beans among four jars, layer each jar with broccoli followed by tomatoes, spinach then grapes, and close the jar with lids. Put in the refrigerator until when you are ready to eat it. Add the dressing and eat from the jar

Mason Jar Quinoa Salad

Servings: 4

Ingredients

Extra virgin olive oil

¼ cup of red onions

1 cup red peppers

½ can of chickpeas

1 cup of red and black beans

1 cup of quinoa

½ cup of kale

½ cucumber

Red wine vinegar

Directions

Start with pouring in the dressing first by combining red wine vinegar and extra virgin oil. Put the ingredients into the jars equally in the order below:

First layer (bottom): chopped red onions

Second layer: cucumbers

Third layer: red peppers

Fourth layer: chickpeas

Fifth layer: red and black beans

Sixth layer: quinoa

Seventh layer (top): kale

Refrigerate then serve.

Mason Jar Chickpea Turkey And Chickpea Vinaigrette

Servings: 4

Ingredients

4 tablespoons of snipped chives

4 heaping tablespoons of dried cherries or raisins

½ cup of chopped tomatoes

1 cup of chickpeas

½ cup of diced cucumber

1 apple, (diced and tossed with fresh lemon)

¼ cup of diced celery

4 tablespoons finely diced red onion

2 cups shredded turkey (pre-cooked)

Pea vinaigrette

Juice of one lemon

4 large mint leaves (chopped)

4 tablespoons water

1 heaping cup of frozen or fresh peas

Salt and pepper

Directions

Put frozen peas and water to warm until the peas are totally defrosted. In a blender, put the peas and dressing ingredients then blend until the mixture is smooth. Meanwhile you will be adding water until the desired consistency is achieved. Also, add salt and pepper while it blends for it to mix uniformly. Divide all the salad ingredients between the jars and put into each jar but leave a half inch space at the top before placing a lid.

Antipasto Salad in a Jar

Servings: 2

What you need

¼ cup of red wine vinegar

½ cup of olive oil

¼ cup of sliced black olives

¼ cup of sliced peperroncini

4 Roma tomatoes

1 head iceberg lettuce (cut in bite-sized pieces)

1/3 pound each of of salami, capicola and mortadella

Salt and pepper

2 wide mouth sized mason jars with lids

Directions

Combine the oil, vinegar, pepper and salt then split equally among the four jars. Divide the tomatoes, pepperoncini and olives uniformly between the two jars. Cut the meat into bit-sized pieces and add ¼ to each jar. Add lettuce into the jar and pack tightly. Put the lids on the jars and put in the refrigerator until ready to serve.

Salads Group #3

Mason Jar Pasta Salad with Avocado Spinach Dressing

Servings: 3

Ingredients

2 tablespoons of kalamata olives

¼ cup of feta cheese

½ cup of cherry tomatoes

½ cup of chopped red bell pepper

½ cup of sliced celery

½ cup of shelled edamame

1 ½ cups of spiraled zucchini

Avocado spinach dressing

¼ teaspoon of pepper

½ teaspoon of salt

2 tablespoons Greek yoghurt (plain 2%)

2 tablespoons extra virgin olive oil

Juice of 1 lemon

½ ripe avocado

½ cup freshly packed spinach

Directions

Shred the zucchini and set aside. Blend the dressing ingredients in a high powered blender until the mixture is smooth. Pour ½ the dressing into the two mason jars. Add the celery to the dressing, and then add peppers on top with edamane. Sprinkle the feta cheese before adding tomatoes and olives. Finally add ½ spiraled zucchini into each of the jar. Refrigerate for at most five days. When serving, shake the jar vigorously before pouring into a plate.

Spring Pea and Romaine With Feta, Cucumber, And Radish salad in a jar

Yield: 2-quarts

Ingredients

2 hearts romaine lettuce (torn)

¼ cup of toasted sunflower

¾ cup of spring peas

½ cup of sliced radishes

¾ cup of sliced cucumbers

¼ cup of crumbled feta cheese

3 tablespoons creamy buttermilk dressing

Directions

Spread 1 ½ tablespoons of salad dressing in the dry quart jar and do this also with the second jar. Crumble two tablespoons of feta to each jar on top of the dressing before adding the radishes, cucumbers and peas. Divide them between the two jars. Lastly top with a lid and refrigerate for a maximum of 5 days.

Arugula, Blueberry and Bacon Salad in a Jar

Servings: 2-quartz

Ingredients

Arugula or spinach

¼ cup of chopped and toasted almonds

¼ cup of cooked and crumbled bacon

1 cup of blueberries (washed and dried)

1 cup of yellow bell pepper (diced)

3 tablespoons of balsamic vinaigrette

Directions

Spread the 1 ½ tablespoons of salad dressing in a jar and do the same with the other jar. Divide the yellow bell pepper and the blueberries equally among the two jars and scatter inside. Add two tablespoons of bacon and the toasted almonds together into the jars. Pack both jars on the remaining space with well dried arugula or spinach and cover with a lid.

Place in the refrigerator and preserve up to 5 days at most.

Buffalo Chicken Jar Salad

Servings: 5

What you need

5 cups of chopped romaine lettuce

10 tablespoons blue cheese yogurt dressing

1 red onion, chopped

1 quart cherry tomatoes (halved)

10 teaspoons of hot sauce (frank sauce preferably)

5 carrots, chopped

¾ cups of shredded chicken

5 celery stalks, chopped

5 wide mouth Mason jar salads

Directions

Split the ingredients among the mason jars beginning with the dressing at the bottom, and then next put in the hot sauce followed by the tomatoes, onions, carrots, celery, chicken and lastly top up with the romaine at the top. Refrigerate until ready to eat for a maximum of 4 days. Shake the jars during serving and pour into a bowl.

Olives Beans Mason Jar Salad

Servings: 4

What you need

4 small sized mason jars with their lids

12 leaves of loose-leaf lettuce

1 cup of pasta (boiled and drained)

1 (15-ounce) can of olives (sliced)

1 (15-ounce) can of garbanzo beans

1 (15-ounce) can of black beans

2 diced tomatoes

½ cup of Italian herb dressing

Directions

Put the ingredients together in layers as in the order given below. Start from the bottom with the Italian herb dressing, then black beans, garbanzo beans, olives, pasta and then finally place the lettuce leaves at the top. Put in the fridge until ready to eat for a maximum of 4 to 5 days.

Caprese Mason Jar Salad

Servings: 4

Ingredients

2 cups of orzo pasta (cooked)

1 cup of baby spinach and basil leaves

2 cups of mixed colored sugar plum tomatoes (yellow, red, orange)

10 ounces of small fresh mozzarella balls

8 tablespoons of balsamic vinaigrette or pesto

Directions

Layer the ingredients in the jars in the following order.

First layer: balsamic vinaigrette or pesto

Second layer: mozzarella balls

Third layer; sugar plum tomatoes

Fourth layer: spinach and basil leaves

Fifth layer: orzo pasta

Make sure you divide all the ingredients evenly among the four jars and shake to coat the ingredients with the dressing.

Salads Group #4

Cobb Mason jar salad

Servings: 4

Ingredients

4 tablespoons blue cheese, crumbled

2 cups of chopped iceberg lettuce

4 tablespoons of green scallions (finely chopped)

2 cups of chopped avocado (tossed in lemon juice to avoid browning)

2 cups of crumbled bacon

4 hard boils eggs (sliced into circles)

2 cups of chopped tomatoes

2 cups of chopped and cooked chicken breasts

8 tablespoons of red wine vinaigrette (ranch or French dressing)

Directions

Put the ingredients in the mason jars in the order below:

First, start with the red wine, lettuce, followed by chicken breasts, tomatoes, boiled eggs, crumbled bacon, avocado, green scallions, and finally crumbled blue cheese at the top. Divide the layering equally among the four jars. Also, shake the salad with the dressing before serving.

Layered Salad with Oil-Free Orange Ginger Dressing

Servings: 4 mason jars

Ingredients

Salad

½ cup of finely chopped fresh parsley

1 ½ cups of diced red pepper

1 cup of edamame

1 cup of uncooked quinoa

1 cup of uncooked wheat berries

1 ½ cups diced green pepper

1 cup diced carrots

Kosher salt to taste

Dressing

1 tablespoon fresh minced ginger

1 tablespoon of apple cider vinegar

1/3 cup of pure apple juice

2/3 cup of 100% pure orange juice

Kosher salt to taste

1 tablespoon fresh lime juice

Directions

Add quinoa and 1 ½ cups of water to a medium–sized pot. Bring to boil then reduce heat to low, cover well and simmer for about 20 minutes. Take care it doesn't burn and then repeat the same process with the wheat berries in a second pot but this time add 2 cups of water and cook until it is tender and chewable. The appropriate cooking time is 5 minutes more than the quinoa. Chop the vegetables then in a jar mix together the dressing and put aside.

When all the grains are well cooked, take the mason jars and put into each of them: ½ cup of wheat berries, followed by ¼ cup of green pepper, ¼ cupful of the red pepper, then ½ cup quinoa, ¼ cup of carrots, 2 tablespoons of parsley, and ¼ cup of edamame in that order to every mason jar. Push it down a bit to have it packed in tightly. When through, keep in the refrigerator until when ready to eat for a maximum of 5 days.

Sprouted spring salad

Servings: 2-500ml Mason jars

Ingredients

1 cup of fresh spring sprouts of your own choice (alfalfa, mustard, clover or onion)

½ cup of pine nuts

1 cup of edamame beans

1 cup of cherry tomatoes (leave them intact instead of slicing them so as to preserve longer)

½ cup of grated carrots

1 cup of cooked chickpeas, (thoroughly rinsed)

Basil vinaigrette

1 heaping teaspoon Dijon mustard

4 chopped basil leaves

2 ½ tablespoons of red wine vinegar

5 tablespoons of olive oil

Sea salt and black pepper to taste

Directions

Combine vinaigrette ingredients in a container with a lid and shake well. Pour basil vinaigrette over chickpeas in a bowl. Normally, the heavier ingredients should be placed first in the jar. Put ½ cup of the chickpea and vinaigrette mixture into each of the mason jars and add all the dressing needed for the salad. Put layers of a half portion carrot followed by the tomato, edamame and then the nuts. Lastly finish by layering the sprouted greens at the top. Close the lids tightly and place in a fridge until ready to use for a maximum of 4 days.

Gazpacho Salad In Jar

Servings: 8

Ingredients

¼ cup of olive oil

½ cup of lemon juice

1 cup of celery stick (thinly sliced)

¾ cup green onions

2 cups of tomato (chopped)

1 medium cucumber (peeled and chopped)

1 cup of green pepper (chopped)

2 cups of lettuce (shredded)

¼ teaspoon of hot sauce

¼ teaspoon of salt

¼ teaspoon of pepper

2 cloves of garlic (minced)

2 teaspoons of Dijon mustard

Directions

Put half of the lettuce, the pepper, the cucumber, the tomato, the celery and the onions in a narrow 2-quartz glass jar with a lid. Mix the remaining ingredients in a jar with a lid then cover and shake thoroughly. Pour the contents over the vegetables and cover for at least 4 hours but keep turning the container occasionally.

Mexican Corn And Bean Salad

Servings: Makes 8 Mason jars

Ingredients

Mexican salad

Cilantro

1 can of black beans

2 avocados

5 vine ripe tomatoes

3 ears of corn

1 yellow pepper

1 red pepper

8 mason Jars

Dressing

1 jalapeno

¾ teaspoon of cumin

1 tablespoon of honey

3 tablespoons of lime juice

3 tablespoons of orange juice

¼ cup of extra virgin olive oil

1 shallot (minced)

Salt and pepper

Directions

Pre-heat oven to 425 °F then cut the peppers into half and place them on a baking sheet. Coat the corn ears and peppers with a couple tablespoons of olive oil and season with freshly ground pepper and salt. Roast them for around 20 minutes rotating the corn after every ten minutes. Make sure the peppers have dark spots. Wait for the peppers to cool down and then peel their skins. Chop them into small pieces. Cut the corn from the cobs and then remove the seeds from the tomatoes, and dice them. Start by layering the corn, peppers and tomatoes into the jar. Rinse and drain the beans and layer them in Mason salad jars.

Dressing

Using a grater, grate the garlic, mince the shallots and jalapeno and add them to the juice before adding the honey and whisking together. Add the olive oil slowly until they are well combined.

Peel and chop both the cilantro and the avocado. Layer the avocado in the jars equally and season with freshly ground pepper and kosher salt. During serving drizzle the dressing over the platter and sprinkle with fresh cilantro.

Salads Group #5

Chicken And Spinach Salad In A Jar

Servings: Makes 4 jars

Ingredients

Mustard-thyme vinaigrette

5 tablespoons of extra virgin olive oil

¼ teaspoon of freshly ground black pepper

¼ teaspoon of kosher salt

¾ teaspoon of chopped fresh thyme leaves

5 teaspoons of country Dijon mustard

5 teaspoons of red wine vinegar

Salad

4 cups of baby spinach, roughly torn

1/3 cup of shaved Asiago cheese

1/3 cup of walnuts (roughly chopped)

2 cups of red grapes (halved)

8 ounces cooked chicken breasts (chopped)

Directions

Start by making your mustard thyme vinaigrette in a small bowl. Do this by whisking together the vinegar, mustard, thyme, salt and pepper. Drizzle slowly with oil while you whisk until it is well combined. Split the vinaigrette equally among 4 mason jars then divide the chicken over the dressing. Put the rest of the ingredients in layers into the jars with the spinach coming last but you will have to squeeze it into the jar to fit tightly. Close the jars with lids and refrigerate for up to 4 days.

Fresh fruit Salad and Lipton Pure Leaf Tea

Servings: 4

Ingredients

1 cup of sliced strawberries

1 peeled and diced honey mango

1 teaspoon lemon juice

1 medium banana (sliced)

1 cup watermelon, diced

Directions

Start by tossing the banana with the lemon juice to ensure it doesn't turn brown then layer the fruits in your own preferred order in 6 (8-ounce) mason jars. Cover and refrigerate up to the time you will be ready to eat. They can last up to 2 days in the refrigerator.

Caprese pasta salad

Servings: 2

Ingredients

½ cup of fresh basil (chopped)

½ cup of fresh spinach leaves

2 ounces of cooked penne pasta

1 ½ ounces of fresh mozzarella (chopped into bite sized pieces)

1 cup of cherry tomatoes

2 tablespoons of basil pesto

Directions

Start arranging the salad in the mason jar starting with the basil pesto then arrange the ingredients in whatever order ending with the spinach at the top.

Taco Salad Jar

Servings: two mason jars

Ingredients

For salad

Sour cream and cheese

Shredded lettuce or any other green leaf

A small handful cilantro

2 tablespoons of fresh salsa

1 small avocado, diced

½ cup of cooked quinoa

¼ cup of sliced green onions

¼ cup of diced red bell pepper

½ cup of black beans (drained and rinsed)

For cumin-lime vinaigrette

½ teaspoon of ground cumin

2 tablespoons of extra virgin olive oil

1 teaspoon honey

A pinch of salt

3 tablespoons of fresh squeezed lime juice

Directions

Whisk all the vinaigrette ingredients and then pour into the quart-sized jars then layer ingredients for the salad in a jar in the following order: the black beans, the diced pepper, the green onions, the quinoa, the avocado, the fresh salsa, the cilantro, the lettuce and lastly the cream at the top. Close with the lid and put in the fridge until when ready to eat. Consume within 3 days.

When serving, turn the jar over the vinaigrette to coat with the salad ingredients.

Chopped Taco Mason Jar Salad

Servings: 5

Ingredients

5 cups of chopped romaine lettuce

1 (1-ounce) jar jalapenos (drained, pickled and chopped)

5 mini cucumbers (sliced)

1 quart cherry tomatoes (halved)

5 tablespoons plain Greek yoghurt

1 ¼ cup of salsa

1 packet of taco seasoning

1 can of black beans drained

1 pound of ground turkey

5 wide mouth quart size mason jars

Directions

Cook ground turkey over medium heat on a pan, until it is no longer pink then add black beans, the seasoning and the amount of water stated in the seasoning instructions. Allow the taco mixture to cool. Split the ingredients among the mason jars starting with the salsa and then add the Greek yoghurt, the tomatoes, the cucumbers, the onions, the jalapenos, the avocados, the taco meat and then the lettuce. Place a lid on and close tightly; do not vacuum seal or anything like that. Shake well when ready to eat then pour into a bowl to serve. It can be served with tortilla chips.

The salads can be made 5 days ahead of time.

Smoked Turkey With Raspberry Vinaigrette And Walnuts

Servings: 5

What you need

5 cups of spring mix and spinach melody

5 tablespoons of chopped raw walnuts

5 tablespoons of crumbled blue cheese

5 hard boiled eggs, peeled and sliced

10 ounces deli turkey breast smoked and sliced

5 baby cucumbers (sliced)

1 quart cherry tomatoes (sliced)

10 tablespoons of vinaigrette dressing (Newman's own Lite Raspberry)

5 (1-quart) wide mouth mason jars

Directions

Split the ingredients between the mason jars and start by layering the dressing in the jars then let it be followed by the tomatoes, then cucumbers, the turkey, the egg, the cheese, and the greens in that order. You should shake well when you are ready to eat before pouring into a bowl. You can keep refrigerated for a maximum of five days before eating.

Salads Group #6

Chopped Turkey and Roasted Red Pepper

Servings: 3

Ingredients

3 cups of romaine lettuce

9 slices of chopped deli turkey

¾ cup of perlini fresh mozzarella balls

18 slices cucumber, (cut into half)

12 cherry tomatoes (cut into half)

Roasted red peppers

3 tablespoons non-fat yoghurt

3 teaspoons of balsamic vinegar

Directions

Split the ingredients equally and assemble the ingredients into each quart Mason jar in the following order: the balsamic vinegar, the yoghurt, the red peppers, the tomatoes, the cucumbers, the mozzarella, the turkey and the lettuce at the top. Close with lid tightly and refrigerator until ready to use for a maximum of five days.

Chopped Broccoli, Ham and Swiss Mason Jar Salad

Servings: 5

What you need

5 cups of spinach, arugula, radicchio and salad blend

5 tablespoons pumpkin seeds

6 ounces of cooked dry spiral whole grain pasta, cooled

½ lb sliced organic deli ham (chopped)

5 ounces Swiss cheese, chopped

3 broccoli crowns (chopped small)

3 large red bell peppers (chopped)

15 tablespoons yoghurt coleslaw dressing

5 wide mouth quart size mason jars

Directions

To the 5 mason jars, pour 3 tablespoons of salad dressing into each and layer the ingredients into the jars starting with the peppers then followed by the broccoli, the ham, the pasta, the cheese, the pumpkin seeds and finish with the salad blend. When serving, toss salad in a bowl and combine the ingredients until they are uniformly coated with the salad dressing.

Artichoke & Tortellini Mason Jar Salad

Servings: 5

What you need

5 cups of bagged spinach or arugula blend salad

5 ounces of goat cheese

4 ounces of dried cheese filled tortellini that is cooked in accordance with the instructions on the package

2 cans of quartered artichoke hearts

1 red onion (chopped)

1 quart cherry tomatoes (halved)

10 tablespoons of Italian dressing

5 quart size wide mouth mason jars

Directions

Put the ingredients in layers into the mason jars starting with the dressing then put in the tomatoes, onion, artichokes, followed by tortellini then goat cheese and finish with arugula or spinach at the top. Shake the jar with the salad before serving.

Chopped Black Bean and Corn Mason Jar Salad

Servings: 5

What you need

¼ cup of cilantro

5 cups of chopped romaine lettuce

5 ounces of block pepper jack cheese (cut into small cubes)

2 avocados (peeled and chopped)

1 (12-ounce) package of frozen corn (thawed)

2 cans of black beans (drained and rinsed)

1 red onion, (chopped)

1 quarts cherry tomatoes (halved)

1 (6-ounce) container plain Greek yoghurt

1 ¼ cup salsa

5 wide mouth quart size Mason jar salads

Directions

Pour ¼ cup of salsa in each one of the jars and then divide the Greek yoghurt evenly among the jars. This will equal about 1 ½ tablespoons of Greek yoghurt per jar. Divide and layer all the other ingredients evenly between the five jars; start with the tomatoes then followed by the onions, the black beans, the corn, the avocado, the cheese, and finish with the romaine and the cilantro. Pour into a bowl when ready to eat. It can be refrigerated up to 5 days.

Layered Cornbread and Turkey Salad

Servings: 6

Ingredients

2 sliced onions

1 (6-ounce) package of buttermilk cornbread mix

10 bacon slices (cooked and crumbled)

2 cups (8-ounces) shredded Swiss cheese

1 cup of diced celery

1 red onion (chopped)

2 large tomatoes (seeded and chopped)

2 large yellow bell peppers (chopped)

2 ½ cups of chopped smoked turkey (3/4 pound)

1 (9 ounce) package romaine lettuce, shredded

¼ cup of buttermilk

½ cup of mayonnaise

1 (12-ounce) of bottle parmesan-peppercorn dressing

Directions

Start by preparing cornbread according to package directions then cool and crumble then put aside. Stir together the dressing, mayonnaise, and buttermilk until blended well. Layer the cornbread, shredded lettuce and the rest of the ingredients evenly into 6 glass jars; spoon half of dressing mixture uniformly on top. Cover and chill for at least 3 hours or up to 24 hours. Sprinkle with green onions just before serving; serve with the remaining half of dressing mixture on the side.

Chickpea Veggie Salad in a Jar

Servings: Fills one 32-ounce jar

Ingredients

Salad

5 ounce chickpeas (rinsed and dried)

4 ounce grape or cherry tomatoes

1 Persian cucumber (chopped)

1 bell pepper (chopped)

½ cup of cooked cold quinoa

1 ounce goat cheese

Dressing

Splash of lemon juice

1 teaspoon white vinegar

3 teaspoons olive oil

Sprinkle of black pepper

Directions

Start by whisking the dressing ingredients in a small bowl, then transfer to the jar. Layer the chickpeas over the dressing and then add tomatoes, followed by cucumber, then bell pepper, quinoa and lastly goat cheese in that order. Secure the lid on tightly until ready to eat. Shake the salad vigorously before tossing it for eating.

Marinated Poppy Seed Strawberry

Servings: 2

What you need

2 mason jars

1 pinch of poppy seeds

1 teaspoon of agave nectar

1 tablespoon of olive oil

1-2 tablespoons balsamic vinegar

1/8 cup feta cheese

¼ cup of pecans/ walnuts

1/8 purple onion

½ cup of strawberries

Organic raw spinach

Directions

Start by quartering the strawberries and removing the stems. If the strawberries happen to be large you can cut them into 8 pieces instead. Shave thin slices of purple onion using a sharp knife or peeler. Combine strawberry, poppy seeds, shaved purple onion, balsamic vinegar, agave nectar, and olive oil in a bowl then stir. Scoop the marinated strawberries into the jar and sprinkle a layer of pecans or walnuts over feta. Fill the remaining spaces with spinach before sealing the containers tightly. Note that this salad is best served after sitting for one day.

Salads Group #7

Chicken Caesar Kale Mason Jar Salad

Servings: 5

Ingredients

For the croutons

½ teaspoon of herbes de Provence

Kosher salt

2 tablespoons of extra virgin olive oil

4 (1-inch) slices day-old crusty bread, cut into small pieces

Dressing

2 cups of extra virgin olive oil

Kosher salt

1 large egg yolk

6 anchovy fillets (olive oil packed)

3 small garlic cloves

2 lemons

For the salad

1 freshly shaved tablespoon parmesan cheese,

3 ounces grilled chicken (cut into chunks)

½ avocado, diced

¼ cup cherry tomatoes

1 cup diced cucumber

2 cups of kale (center stems, removed and leaves torn into small pieces)

Directions

To make the croutons, start by pre-heating your oven to about 400°F and then using olive oil, toss the bread, a pinch of salt, and the herbes de Provence in a medium bowl. Spread the bread evenly on a baking sheet and bake until golden brown and crisp for about 15 minutes. In the mid of the baking time, redistribute the croutons if you notice that they are coloring un-uniformly. Let the croutons cool down.

Dressing

Grate the zest from 1 lemon and then cut both lemons into halves. Place the anchovies, garlic, and the lemon zest in a blender and run the blender until a thick paste is formed. Put in the egg yolks followed by a pinch of salt then squeeze the juice of lemon and pulse until they are well combined. Run the blender on low speed as you pour in ½ cup of the olive oil drop by drop. Do this until the mixture is thick and creamy. Stop periodically pouring the oil and add a squeeze of lemon. Taste the dressing before adding more lemon juice and salt. Add water, a small spoonful at a time, blending to thin the dressing to the creamy consistency.

Making the salad

Mix two tablespoons of dressing with the chopped kale and cucumbers in a bowl and toss to coat. Add the cucumbers and the kale to a quart sized wide mouth mason jar. Add the cherry tomatoes followed by the diced avocado, the chicken and then the parmesan and then put a square parchment paper across top, put in the croutons and seal. Refrigerate for a maximum of 4 days if you are not ready to use immediately.

Rainbow Spinach Salad

Servings: 4

What you need

½ cup of your favorite vinaigrette dressing

1 cup of fresh tomatoes (diced)

1 orange bell pepper (diced)

2/3 cup of fresh or frozen corn niblets

3 cups of chopped fresh spinach

2/3 cup of chopped purple cabbage

4 small-sized Mason jar salads

Directions

Put the salad in a mason jar, beginning with the cabbage at the bottom, spinach followed by corn, diced bell pepper and lastly top it with tomatoes. Drizzle the dressing on the salad and cover the Mason jar with a lid. Shake the salad vigorously to mix the dressing.

Mason Jar Greek Salad with Chickpeas

Servings: 1

What you need

For the salad

2 tablespoons of chopped fresh parsley

2 ounces of crumbled feta cheese

2 tablespoons of pitted black olives (halved)

2 tablespoons of diced red onions

1/3 cup of quartered cucumber slices

1/3 cup of halved cherry tomatoes

½ cup of chickpeas, rinsed and drained

2 tablespoons of lemon vinaigrette

For the lemon vinaigrette

3 tablespoons of olive oil

Freshly ground black pepper (to taste)

A pinch of salt

Juice of one lemon

1 Mason jar

Directions

In making the salad

To the Mason jar, layer the vinaigrette and add the chick peas then put layers of olives, feta cheese, cucumber, cherry tomatoes, onion and finally parsley. Close with the lid and put in the fridge until when you will eat the salad.

For the vinaigrette

Start by mixing juice of the lemon, salt and pepper then slowly put in the olive oil while still mixing until the dressing thickens.

Mason Jar Layered Bean Dip

Servings: 6

Ingredients

½ cup of green scallions (thinly sliced)

½ cup of mini colored cherry tomatoes (chopped)

3 ounce can of sliced black olives

1 cup of shredded cheddar cheese

1 cup of fresh chunky salsa

1 cup of guacamole

1 pint of sour cream

1 (16 ounce) can salsa-style friend pinto beans

Directions

Place the pinto beans from the can in a bowl and mix. Spread the beans in the mason jars and spread the sour cream over the beans. This should be followed by the guacamole and then the salsa. Follow this by adding cheese, olives, tomatoes and lastly scallions. When serving, serve this with tortilla chips.

Strawberry Pecan Salad

Servings: 4

Ingredients

4 tablespoons of candied pecans (chopped)

Spinach (washed and completely dried)

4 tablespoons goat cheese

9 small-medium strawberries (sliced)

1 diced avocado

½ English cucumber (diced)

1 cup of quinoa (cooked)

Lemon poppy salad dressing

Directions

Start with a layer of two tablespoons of lemon poppy seed dressing then ¼ cup of the quinoa, cucumber, the diced avocado, a layer of sliced strawberries and 1 tablespoon of goat cheese. Add the dried spinach and then one tablespoon of pecans. Cover with a lid. Toss and serve.

Greek Salad In A Jar With Chickpeas And Feta Cheese

Servings: 3

Ingredients

Lettuce

6 tablespoons of feta cheese

1 (15-ounce) can of chickpeas; rinsed and drained

12 halved cherry tomatoes

¼ red onion (diced)

½ English cucumbers (diced)

Greek-style dressing or homemade Greek dressing

Directions

Start by spreading two tablespoons of the Greek-style salad dressing in 3 mason jars. Put in the cucumber followed by red onion then cherry tomatoes, chickpeas and finally feta cheese in that order splitting the ingredients among the three jars. Pack a handful of lettuce tightly into each jar and cover them.

Conclusion

As you have noticed, preparing mason jar salads is quite simple. As you embrace making more mason jar salads, you will also get to take more vegetables as the recipes above are quite tasty. Now you don't have any reason for not carrying some packed salad to work.

Your next step is to start exploring with the mason jar salads provided and see which one becomes your favorite. I would also recommend that you check out my other book titled **"Mason Jar Meals: Amazingly Delicious and Easy To Make Recipes For Meals On The Go"** It will be the perfect complement to this book to add some great meals and variety to your daily routine.

I have included a free preview on the next page for your viewing pleasure.

Thanks

Sara Banks

Free Preview Mason Jar Meals

Polenta with Cream Cheese and Chives

Servings: 6 pint-sized mason jars

Ingredients

2 tablespoons of chives (chopped)

6 tablespoons of cream cheese

1 cup of yellow cornmeal

1 teaspoon of salt

4 cups of water

Directions

Bring water and salt to boil in a medium sauce pan, and then add the cornmeal slowly as you continue whisking. Lower the heat to low and then simmer for about 10 minutes and keep stirring constantly until it is thick. Remove from the heat and stir it in cream cheese and the chives until it is fully combined. Divide the mixture between six mason jars of pint size then let it cool and refrigerate to set.

Irish Shepherd's Pie

Servings: six wide mouth mason jars

Ingredients

For malcannon topping

1/8 teaspoon of freshly ground nutmeg

¾ teaspoon of salt

1 ½ tablespoons of butter

¾ cup of milk

1 leek (sliced) light green and white parts only

3 cups of packed chopped kale (de-stemmed)

3 medium Yukon gold potatoes (1 pound)

For the filling

¼ cup of chopped parsley (flat- leaf)

1 cup of frozen peas (thawed)

2 teaspoons of vegetarian Worcestershire

½ cup of vegetable broth

½ cup of Guinness

2 tablespoons of flour

½ teaspoon of freshly ground pepper

½ teaspoon of salt

1 bay leaf

1 cup of chopped cabbage

2 medium carrots (finely chopped)

3 finely chopped leaves of celery

2 cloves of garlic, minced

1 medium onion (chopped)

1 ½ tablespoons of olive oil (divided)

14 ounces of crumbled vegetarian sausage

Directions

Pre-heat an oven to heat of 400°F.

Meanwhile prepare the colcannon:

Start by peeling the potatoes then chop them into large cubes. Put them in a medium sized pot and cover the pot with water. Over high heat, bring to a simmer then reduce heat to low. Simmer for about 15 minutes until the potatoes break apart when poked with a spoon. Drain the potatoes then return them to pot and mash them before covering.

As the potatoes are cooking, bring the leek, the kale, the milk, the salt, the butter and the nutmeg to a simmer in a pot. Let it remain covered and stir from time to time until soft for about 12 minutes. Add kale mixture to mashed potatoes and the sir to incorporate. Let it remain covered as you prepare the filling.

Prepare Filling:

Heat 1 tablespoon of the olive oil in a pan on medium-high heat. Once the oil is hot, add the sausage and cook until browned. Put the sausage aside in a plate. Place half tablespoon of olive oil in the same pan used for sausage and add garlic, onion, carrot, celery, bay leaf, cabbage, salt and pepper. Sauté for 12 minutes until it is soft then add flour and stir until the veggies are uniformly coated. Add the Guinness, Worcestershire and the broth then cook until bubbly and thick. Put the sausage, the parsley and the peas then continue cooking until well co.............

Made in the USA
Lexington, KY
04 November 2014